**At the
Top of
Their
Game**

Mookie Betts

Baseball Record-Breaker

Budd Bailey

Cavendish Square

New York

Published in 2020 by Cavendish Square Publishing, LLC
243 5th Avenue, Suite 136, New York, NY 10016

Library of Congress Cataloging-in-Publication Data

Names: Bailey, Budd, 1955- author.
Title: Mookie Betts : baseball record-breaker / Budd Bailey.
Description: First edition. | New York : Cavendish Square, 2020. | Series: At the top of
their game | Audience: Grades: 9 to 12. | Includes bibliographical references and index.
Identifiers: LCCN 2019009298 (print) | LCCN 2019013344 (ebook) |
ISBN 9781502651075 (ebook) | ISBN 9781502651068 (library bound)
| ISBN 9781502651044 (pbk.) | ISBN 9781502651051 (6 pack)
Subjects: LCSH: Betts, Mookie, 1992-—Juvenile literature. | Baseball
players—United States—Biography—Juvenile literature.
Classification: LCC GV865.B488 (ebook) | LCC GV865.B488
B35 2020 (print) | DDC 796.357092 [B] —dc23
LC record available at https://lccn.loc.gov/2019009298

Editor: Jodyanne Benson
Copy Editor: Michele Suchomel-Casey
Associate Art Director: Alan Sliwinski
Designer: Joe Parenteau
Production Coordinator: Karol Szymczuk
Photo Research: J8 Media

Printed in China

At the Top of Their Game

Contents

Big Enough

It was the start of the third inning of the last game of the 2018 regular season for the Boston Red Sox, and the fans were in a festive mood. They had watched their favorite team have the greatest regular season in its history, as Boston was on its way to its 108th win.

At that point, Red Sox manager Alex Cora sent utility player Tzu-Wei Lin out to right field so that star outfielder Mookie Betts could receive one more standing ovation as he left the game and ended his regular season. Betts's departure from Game 162 meant that he officially had won the American League batting championship with a .346 average—the first Red Sox player to do so since Wade Boggs in 1988.

Most Valuable Player

However, the fans wanted more for Mookie, so they chanted "M-V-P" as he left the field. Betts, they thought, was the clear choice for the Most Valuable Player (MVP) Award in the American

Opposite: Mookie Betts emerged as one of baseball's best players in 2018.

The 2018 season proved unforgettable for Mookie. Not only did he win many individual awards, but he led the Boston Red Sox to a World Series championship.

League—the greatest individual honor that a player can win in a season. Teammate J. D. Martinez, who also was under consideration for MVP honors, would have voted for his teammate.

"If he's not your MVP, I don't know who is," Martinez said after the game. "He's as good as advertised."

Betts was the first batting champion to lead the major leagues in batting average while compiling thirty home runs and stealing thirty bases. The outfielder also became the first American League player to lead the majors in both batting average and extra-base hits since

Mickey Mantle did it in 1956. In the clubhouse after his shortened workday, Betts was busy looking forward to the postseason instead of looking backward at his regular season.

"If that time comes and if I'm able to win it," Betts said of the MVP Award, "then cool. If not, no worries. I'm worried about the World Series right now."

As we later learned, Betts would be collecting awards, trophies, and honors for the rest of 2018. When he won that Most Valuable Player vote, the young star became the third Red Sox player to be a batting champion and MVP award winner in the same year. Ted Williams, considered one of the greatest hitters in baseball history, never did it. Only Carl Yastrzemski and Jimmie Foxx completed that double.

In addition, the Red Sox won the World Series, which for Betts, capped one of the greatest individual seasons in baseball history. When a list of baseball's best players is compiled in the near future, Mookie Betts's name almost assuredly will be on it.

Small for a Superstar

For the most part, Betts's superstar status isn't a great surprise to those who have followed his athletic accomplishments over the years. He's always been great in everything he does, mixing athletic ability with a drive to work on all parts of his game in order to get better. That's something of a common element with the all-time greats.

However, Betts has had some doubters along the way, and it's because of one particular measurement—size. Betts always has been on the small side, but he has been proving that he belongs with the best throughout his life—starting at the age of five. He eventually

Phil Rizzuto wasn't a particularly big man for a professional athlete, but that small body contained plenty of talent. The New York Yankees' shortstop is a member of baseball's Hall of Fame.

Mookie Betts: Baseball Record-Breaker

reached a height of 5 feet 9 inches (1.8 meters) and180 pounds (82 kilograms). Baseball scouts prefer their prospects to be big and strong like Mike Trout, the sensational outfielder for the Los Angeles Angels. He is 6 feet 3 inches tall (1.9 m) and 235 pounds (107 kg). Even future teammate Xander Bogaerts didn't give Betts a second look when he saw him for the first time in 2011. "He was short," Bogaerts said. "I didn't think much of him. I was not impressed."

History teaches us that while it's difficult for a comparatively small player to win an MVP trophy, it's still possible. The 5 foot 2 (1.7 m) Phil Rizzuto of the New York Yankees was the American League's best in 1950, and the 5 foot 9 (1.8 m) Dustin Pedroia—Betts's teammate with the Red Sox—took home MVP honors in 2008. In 2017, José Altuve of the Houston Astros won the league's top honor. He is only 5 feet 6 inches (1.7 m) tall, but his batting average was .346 with twenty-four home runs. Then came Mookie.

"Mookie's size doesn't matter," teammate Andrew Benintendi said to ESPN in 2018. "It's all about how you use what you have."

Let's go back in time almost three decades and tell the story about how Mookie Betts went from "too small" to "too good."

Chapter 1

From Markus to Mookie

B y the time Game Six of the 1986 World Series had ended, no one would have believed that someone nicknamed "Mookie" would someday become a hero of Boston sports fans.

In the bottom of the tenth inning on an October night in Shea Stadium in New York, the Boston Red Sox led the New York Mets, 5–3. Two men were out, and no one was on base. Surely the Red Sox were about to become World Series champions for the first time since 1918, a sixty-eight-year drought between titles that was one of the longest in baseball history. The Red Sox had a three-games-to-two lead, and their chances of winning Game Six and the series were estimated by analysts at 99 percent.

Then, Gary Carter, Kevin Mitchell, and Ray Knight singled for the Mets, narrowing the gap to 5–4. Bob Stanley came on to pitch in relief, and the first batter he faced was named "Mookie"—Mookie Wilson, with a real first name of William. Stanley had thrown a wild pitch that allowed Mitchell to score the tying run from third. Then,

Opposite: Mookie Wilson's ground ball helped turn near-certain defeat into victory for the New York Mets in their 1986 World Series win over the Boston Red Sox.

Wilson hit a ground ball to first baseman Bill Buckner, who had the ball skip under his glove and into right field. Knight scored from second, and the Mets had miraculously evened the series.

New York went on to win the seventh game and the championship two days later. The ground ball involving Buckner and Wilson became a symbol of Boston's long wait to win a World Series banner—one that didn't end until 2004.

Welcome, Mookie

About eight years after that game, on October 7, 1992, a boy named Markus Lynn Betts was born in Nashville, Tennessee. His parents were Willie Betts (whose middle name, Mark, was lengthened to Markus for his son) and wife Diana (who middle name is Lynn). Markus came from an active family. His dad, a railroad mechanic and Vietnam War veteran, ran track and played basketball in his youth. His mom loved to bowl and was a good softball player in high school. In addition, baseball might have been in the back of his parents' minds when Markus arrived. His initials were MLB—just like Major League Baseball.

As for the nickname, Diana was a fan of professional basketball player Daron "Mookie" Blaylock, who was in the midst of a 13-year career when Markus was born that saw him average almost 13 points per game. Diana thought it would be a great name for her son, and "Mookie" became the name of choice. The former Markus has stuck with "Mookie" throughout his life.

"Mookie didn't go straight from the crib to the fields of play, but it was close," Diana said to MassLive.com. "Mookie liked anything and everything that involved a ball. If it involved a ball, he played it and he loved it. He just liked playing; he's competitive."

Mookie Blaylock had a fine career as a professional basketball player over thirteen years. His nickname lives on because of Mookie Betts.

At five years old, he thought he was ready to try baseball. After all, his mother's cousin was Terry Shumpert—then in the midst of a fourteen-year major-league career that included a brief stop in Boston. Diana and Mookie went off to a Nashville elementary school to register him for organized baseball, as they heard a youth team was looking for players. However, a coach took one look at Mookie and decided he was too small to play on his team.

"I mean, he was the skinniest little thing," Diana said to the *Tennessean*. "He looked like he couldn't catch or do anything. The coach said, 'Sorry, I have enough small kids. I can't take him.' So I gathered up all of the kids nobody wanted and we started our own team."

Thanks, Mom

Mookie Betts's first baseball coach, then, was his mother. The youngster needed suspenders to keep his pants up, but he could play. "For me, it was very enjoyable because my mom was competitive the same way I was," he said to the *Sporting News*. "She was into the games, trying to win. She instilled in me, 'Hey, we're trying to win the game even though we're young.'"

Even at the age of five, Mookie was a standout. At one point, he was about the only player on his team capable of recording an out in the field, since no one else on his team could catch the ball, so Diana told him to make an out any way he could, if only to move the game along. Mookie followed orders. When the next ball was hit to him in the infield, Mookie caught it and ran to first—just beating the runner there to record an out.

The other team complained that Mookie wasn't playing the game correctly, but the coach disagreed. "Boy, you did a good job,"

Diana said. "You are so fast and momma is so proud of you. You did everything right."

At a young age, it seemed like almost nothing could stop Mookie Betts—with one exception. "If someone hit a snake or a raccoon [while driving], you'd tell Mookie and he'd start crying," Willie Betts said to the *Tennessean* with a laugh. "He could do all these things. One thing he couldn't do is look at a dead animal on the road."

Trying It All

Mookie tried everything in the world of sports, and he was good at everything—basketball, soccer, football, and bowling. He could even beat adults in table tennis. His parents split up when he was ten, and Diana remarried. However, Mookie's parents worked together when it came to helping their son achieve athletic success.

Years later, Mookie believes switching from sport to sport only helped him reach the status that he has today. He believes any young person who has hopes of playing at a sport's highest level should do the same thing. "Play all the sports. Don't just play baseball," he said to ESPN.com. He went on to explain:

> You're kind of limiting yourself. You don't really know what you're going to end up doing, so I would advise to get into all sports and see how that treats you. I played multiple sports until I graduated: baseball, basketball, football. I played one year of soccer. I bowled. All that stuff.
>
> I stopped playing football at 14, and the only reason I stopped was because my mom said I was too small to keep playing. I really worked on

There weren't many sports that Mookie Betts didn't try as a kid, and he seemed to be good at all of them.

basketball, though. I played way more basketball than I did baseball growing up. I loved basketball. I kind of wanted that to be my sport. But baseball is the sport I was the best at.

It didn't take long for other people to figure out that when it came to hand-eye coordination, Mookie was in a class by himself. At about ten years old, he was participating in a youth baseball camp at the University of Tennessee when he was thrown a pitch near the dirt. Mookie adjusted his swing and hit a line drive on a pitch that he had no business touching, let alone hitting hard. Coach Rod Delmonico of the Volunteers ordered the pitcher to throw the same pitch. The result was the same—line drive.

When the day's activities were over, Delmonico made sure to talk to Willie Betts. "Your son needs to play baseball," the coach said.

No can ever know for sure what might happen to such athletic prodigies, no matter how much potential they show as a child. We can say, though, that when Mookie Betts was twelve years old, something that happened that put everything in perspective for him and his family.

Overcoming a Car Accident

Mookie was riding in a vehicle driven by his stepfather between Nashville and Kansas City when it collided with a pole and rolled on to a median. Mookie was ejected from the car. A stranger picked him up and carried him to safety. "My mom said if the cars kept on going, they probably would have rolled over me," he told Boston.com.

Mookie's injuries were not insignificant. He suffered a dislocated wrist, some broken toes, and some damage to his jaw. However, it could have been much worse, and it didn't slow him down for long. In spite of a cast, Mookie soon returned to baseball to serve as an extra hitter. He connected a batting glove to his cast and came out swinging. Even Mookie didn't know how he could play in games that way, but he found a way to make it work.

Finding a Role Model

By this time, Terry Shumpert was starting to play an ever-growing role in Mookie's life. Mookie was lucky enough to have a major leaguer in the family who could be a role model. Shumpert brought his son Nick and Mookie to Colorado one time in the early 2000s when Shumpert was playing with the Rockies. The two kids had the chance to take batting practice at Coors Field.

Mookie's cousin was destined to be drafted by the Atlanta Braves and play minor league baseball and in independent, international baseball leagues as of 2019. Mookie was four years older and more fully developed at that stage of his life. A few swings in the Rockies' batting cage and Shumpert was convinced about Mookie's chances of becoming a good player someday. "I went back home and told my wife, 'He's got that swing. He's got that swing,'" Shumpert told SBNation.com.

The family ties between Shumpert and Betts grew

Terry Shumpert played more than eight hundred games in the major leagues during his fourteen-year career.

From Markus to Mookie

closer in 2006. Shumpert spent his last season as a professional player, by chance, in Nashville, as the Pittsburgh Pirates had their Triple-A team there. Mookie had the chance to spend time around excellent players and see what was needed to reach that level. "When Mookie came out, and I'm sure he was aware of it at the time, he saw the grind," Shumpert said. He added:

> I was always the happiest guy around because I was playing the major leagues and this is always what I wanted to do as a kid. Even if I was there for parts of 14 seasons, it was always the greatest thing in the world. I think that Mookie couldn't help but to see that. I wasn't one of those kids raised around baseball and clubhouses. Those kids [that are raised that way]— the maturity, the calmness, the mindset that those kids show—is a huge help for them. It's a big benefit.

The sports world is filled with young athletes who do remarkable things as children. Then, they arrive at high school and those "can't miss" prospects begin to miss for one reason or another. Maybe they get hurt, or maybe they discover that their skills aren't good enough to compete with the area's best. Even so, you'd have to think that Mookie Betts had some confidence that he could play with anyone when he first walked through the doors of John Overton High School in Nashville.

Overton High is mostly known for its music program. It has won several championships in national and regional competitions. The marching band has appeared at the Macy's Thanksgiving Day Parade and the Tournament of Roses Parade.

In athletics, the Bobcats—Overton's mascot—have won state championships in a variety of sports over the years. The school has had a few professional athletes pass through its corridors, including baseball's Sam Ewing—a member of the original Toronto Blue Jays team in 1977—and football's Jeff Gooch.

It turned out that it took Mookie little time to make an impact. He wasn't allowed to play football by his mother, even though he had so much athletic ability that a coach thought he might have been an all-state quarterback had he played. However, Mookie was a big part of the baseball and basketball teams at Overton. The signs of greatness started to show at an early age.

For example, Mookie hadn't even reached his full height of 5 foot 9 (1.8 m) when he was a high school sophomore. He received some good-natured taunting from his baseball and basketball teammate Quinn Anderson about his inability to dunk a basketball. Then, during a game, Mookie made a slam dunk that left everyone in the building shocked. Mookie simply looked at Quinn and said, "Yeah."

Later that school year, Mookie was playing in a state playoff baseball game. He came to the plate with his team down four runs and the bases loaded. Mookie launched a rocket down the left field line.

His teammates, who were on the top of the steps in the dugout, became so excited that they actually pulled the fence protecting them from foul balls out of the ground. Their joy turned to disappointment when the left fielder made a game-saving catch at the wall, but Mookie had shown that the other team was always in a difficult situation when he was at the plate.

Mookie Betts is only one of many fine athletes who have walked through the doors of John Overton High School.

A Double-Header Day

In the meantime, Mookie hadn't stopped participating in other sports. He still turned up at Nashville-area bowling lanes, and he was clearly the best bowler in the school. How could he be on the bowling and the basketball teams at the same time, though, since they were both winter sports?

The coaches of those respective teams got together and came up with an answer. Mookie couldn't practice with the bowling team because that would interfere with basketball practice, but he could take part in matches.

On one particular day in his high school career, Mookie broke 250 in an afternoon bowling match, which is impressively close to a perfect game of 300. Then, he headed for the basketball court, and he scored 18 points with 7 assists and 4 steals, leading the Overton Bobcats to a win.

Table tennis wasn't an interscholastic sport, but he probably could have been all-state in that. When Overton added a Ping-Pong table to its recreational supplies, Mookie was ready to take on all comers. "He beat me in ping-pong while talking on the phone with his girlfriend," Chris Hight, one of Mookie's basketball coaches, told overthemonster.com. "I told him I was never playing with him ever again. The boy is good at everything he does."

With all that going on, Mookie still needed something to do in the fall. He wasn't a part of any team, but his friends were on the football team. The solution was simple: join the team as a manager. "I spent four years as water boy because all my friends played," Betts told WEEI Radio.

> I was the real water boy. I traveled with the team. I was always there. All my friends played and it was a way to be around it. I had no shame in it. Sometimes when I was walking around people would make jokes, but I didn't care.
>
> I filled up all the water bottles. I made sure everybody had what they needed. If they needed something out of the locker, I got it. If they needed something with the buttons on their chin straps I took care of it. But I got to be around all my buddies and got in the games for free.

There was one other advantage to his connection to the football team: access to the weight room. Mookie was never going to be a huge man, but he had the chance to develop his muscles in the fall. After all, he was rather busy during the rest of the school year.

The Big Finish

Mookie kept up that schedule for the rest of his days in high school. For those who like numbers, Mookie turned in a pair of fabulous baseball seasons. He hit .549 with 6 home runs, 37 runs batted in (RBIs), and 24 stolen bases as a junior.

It was more of the same as a senior—.509 with 25 extra-base hits, 39 RBIs, and 29 stolen bases—while splitting time between shortstop, second base, and center field. As a senior, Mookie was placed on the honorable mention list for the Louisville Slugger High School All-American team.

During that final season, Overton was involved in a close regular-season game and needed a pitcher. The head coach waved Mookie in from the infield and handed him the ball. Mookie threw most of the pitches around 85 miles per hour (136.8 kilometers per hour) and had a nice curve ball.

"On the hill [another name for the pitcher's mound], that's when I really saw his competitive spirit," teammate Quinn Anderson said to overthemonster.com. "When they ended up pulling him out of the game, he ended up crying just because he couldn't do it anymore."

In basketball, Mookie was the Most Valuable Player in his district as a senior. He averaged 14.4 points, 5.8 assists, and 2.4 steals. Even being relatively short, he might have become a top college point guard had he gone that route. "His basketball IQ was so far above everyone else's," Hight said. "I was the offensive coach, so I could run a play or set up a play and he already knew what I was going to do in advance. He always helped me get the other kids in the right position and help them be successful also."

Meanwhile, on the bowling lanes, Mookie finished third in the Tennessee State Championship as a junior, and he earned the boys' Bowler of the Year Award. By graduation, he had a pair of perfect games and an 800 total for a three-game series.

Mookie didn't spend all his free time playing sports, as he did some studying along the way as well. He had a 3.5 grade point average (GPA), despite taking some advanced placement (AP) classes. There was no one better at solving a Rubik's Cube—he could do it in about two minutes. It's a skill he maintains to this day.

High school couldn't have gone much better for Mookie Betts. Now, it was time to determine what his next step would be. He would have to choose between two different paths.

Chapter 2

Two Paths to the Future

By the time he was ready to graduate from high school in 2011, Mookie Betts probably had figured out that professional baseball was in his future. The scouts from major league teams who had watched him at his games were the most obvious sign of that. Still, Betts had the biggest decision of his young life right in front of him. Would he play college baseball, or would he immediately sign with a major league team?

He knew he probably would be offered hundreds of thousands of dollars to skip college and become a professional. That would be very tempting at the age of seventeen. Betts had to figure out exactly how much money would make it worthwhile to play baseball immediately.

A Tough Decision

Baseball's rules are different than the other major sports' laws about turning professional. In basketball, players are allowed to enter the National Basketball Association (NBA) draft a year after they

Opposite: It took some time for Mookie Betts to adjust as he climbed the ladder in minor league baseball.

graduate from high school. Most players who are considered the best in their class go to college for a year, and then they head to the NBA. In football, potential players must be out of high school for three years and have used up their college eligibility in order to be eligible for the National Football League (NFL). They do have the option of applying to enter the draft a year early.

In baseball, there are two different paths to the professional ranks. A player may be picked and signed by a major league team right out of high school. If he chooses not to sign a contract and enters college, he has to wait until he is twenty-one years old and finished with his junior season to become eligible to be drafted again. If a high school player is drafted by an MLB team but not signed by August 15, the team loses its rights to sign him.

Betts, therefore, had some leverage in contract negotiations. The University of Tennessee offered him a baseball scholarship. If Betts wasn't offered a satisfactory amount of money, he could go to college and wait three years to be picked again.

Boston Red Sox scout Danny Watkins had been watching Betts quite closely during his high school career, and he wanted Boston to draft him badly.

"Whether he was pulling the ball or hitting the ball the other way, he always seemed to find a way to put the barrel on the ball," Watkins said to ESPN. "He rarely offered at pitches that were outside the zone, and when he did, he very seldom swung and missed. And when you see the athleticism, there was a degree of explosiveness to him, whether it was in his hands, in his feet or just his overall actions."

One time, Watkins took Betts and his mother to a Cracker Barrel restaurant to discuss the future. "You're talking about potentially changing or altering this kid's direction in life," Watkins said to MassLive.com. He further explained:

> Since the time he was young, the thinking is: high school, college, then a profession. So you're talking about giving them the chance to alter that and so you really want to focus in more on their family life, their home life, how stable has it been, how mature is this guy going to be when he gets out on his own—and all of the sudden he's responsible for cleaning his own clothes and responsible for finding his own meals.

A professional career in sports changes someone's life. Betts would have to transition into adulthood quickly. The decision between college and a professional sports career is not always easy. Betts had a lot of factors to consider in his deliberation.

Caught in the Draft

Betts had one other issue that was part of his situation in 2011. Major League Baseball had agreed to a new compensation plan starting in 2012 that would tie contracts for drafted players to where they were picked. If a team's total spending on new players for the year went over its allotment, it would face a tax from Major League Baseball. However, there was no such tax in 2011. The Red Sox were very prepared to be aggressive with their spending on 2011 draft picks.

Boston took Matt Barnes, Blake Swihart, and Jackie Bradley with their first three picks. All were on the team's 2018 World Series roster. On draft day, Betts's mom followed the selections by computer while he played video games in the den. A total of 171

Matt Barnes was part of the great Red Sox draft of 2011 that supplied several players for the team's championship roster of 2018.

players were chosen before Betts was taken by the Red Sox in the fifth round. Betts simply talked to his agent and went upstairs to his room. The reaction in Boston wasn't too emotional, either.

"It wasn't like we all turned to each other and said, 'I can't believe we got Mookie Betts in the fifth round!'" Amiel Sawdaye, Red Sox amateur scouting director, said to ESPN. "If we thought Mookie Betts was going to be what he is, we would've taken him in the first round."

The Red Sox soon turned their focus to their eighth-round pick, Senquez Golson of Mississippi. He was a first-team high school All-American in baseball, and he was considered a great all-around athlete who was one of the nation's best high school football cornerbacks. The team offered Golson more than $1 million to sign with them, but Golson decided to attend the University of Mississippi, where he became an All-American football player and a second-round NFL draft choice. Boston then had enough money in its budget to sign Betts for a $750,000 bonus shortly before the deadline.

There wasn't much time left in the 2011 baseball season when Betts agreed to terms. He joined the Red Sox rookie team in the Gulf Coast League (GCL), and he got in the lineup for one game. Betts had his first hit as a professional, but he also finished with three errors at shortstop.

That was it for professional baseball for several months. In the summer of 2012, Betts was assigned to play with the Lowell Spinners of the New York–Penn League, which was filled with players who had just finished high school. Betts led the team in games played with 71. He started the season at shortstop but moved over to second to make room for 2012 first-round pick Devan Marrero. The Nashville native knew he had some work to do early in that season. "It's just the speed of the game and everybody being on the same talent level," Betts said to the *Tennessean* about professional baseball after hitting .225 in his first 10 games in Lowell. "It's kind of a big difference."

No one would have guessed that Betts would be a major-league star at that point. He did lead Lowell in runs batted in with 31. His speed also earned some attention, but he only hit .267 with no home runs. It was far too early to give up on a 19-year-old, 156-pound (71 kg) young man who was still finding his way in the game.

However, even Betts was having doubts as he struggled through his first professional season. He frequently talked with his friends back home for support. "He would call us every day morning and night," friend Cameron Lewis said. "Like, 'I don't know if I can get used to this, I don't know if I can do this.' That's when he really needed us."

A writer for Soxprospects.com put it this way at the end of the season: "Power will not be a part of the 20-year-old's game, but he has the bat speed and type of compact stroke to round into a gap-to-gap line drive hitter… Betts shows the ability to get the bat on the ball, but it is often weaker contact when he puts the ball into play."

Mookie Betts needed time to learn, grow, and get used to the higher level of play before finding his way in professional baseball.

Two Paths to the Future

Another Slow Start

The problems continued through the first month of baseball in Class A ball, as he played for the Greenville (South Carolina) Drive in the South Atlantic League. Betts finished April 2013 with a .157 average. At that point, someone who had everything athletic come easily to him was faced with the possibility of failure. Betts even called his relative, Terry Shumpert, and asked if he could be sent to a lower classification.

"Mookie, they don't send guys down from Low-A," Shumpert said he told Betts. "If you were hitting .140 in Boston, they may consider sending you down, but Mookie, I know you're fine. You're either gonna [sic] hit .200 this year or you're gonna [sic] get it together. You're not going anywhere."

That was reassuring, and so was the presence of family and friends at the Drive's games. Greenville was about a five-hour ride from Nashville, much closer than Lowell, so Betts frequently had his own cheering section. Soon, Betts started to hit the ball hard, and he played with confidence.

The turnaround was dramatic. Betts finished his 76-game stay in Greenville with a .296 batting average, 8 home runs, 26 RBIs, and 18 stolen bases. That earned the second baseman a spot on the league all-star team and a promotion to Salem of the Carolina League. There, he hit .341 with 7 home runs and 39 RBIs in only 51 games. In other words, Betts played like a top prospect for the first time. Betts also played well in the fall of 2013 in the Arizona Instructional League. He was named the Red Sox Minor League Offensive Player of the Year.

As Betts gained confidence in the minor leagues, he began to stand out as a potential star.

Two Paths to the Future

Everyone who paid attention to minor league baseball noticed what Betts had done. Several organizations ranked him as one of the 100 best prospects in baseball. Fangraphs.com put him at No. 59, ESPN placed him at No. 61, MLB.com had him at No. 62, and Baseball America ranked him at No. 75. Now, the Red Sox started to wonder where Betts might play once he arrived in the majors. The Red Sox already had Dustin Pedroia, an All-Star, at second base. Luckily, Betts had shown that he had the athletic ability to try another position—such as the outfield.

Too Good for the League

The next step was up to Double-A baseball, as Betts was assigned to the Double-A Portland (Maine) Sea Dogs of the Eastern League in the spring of 2014. Double-A often separates the prospects from the suspects. Betts showed right away that he was a prospect by hitting an almost absurd .402 for the first month of the season.

"I'm a little bit surprised, but I do know that it's only the first month of the season, and I have five more months to go," Betts said to the *Tennessean*. "I could hit .430 for that one month and could hit .130 this month. I just try to stay on an even keel."

His batting average "slid" to only .355 after 54 games with the Sea Dogs. Betts drove in 34 runs and stole 22 bases in that time. He had nothing to prove in Double-A. On June 3, it was on to the Triple-A Pawtucket (Rhode Island) Red Sox in the International League.

"I think at some point, we have an obligation to challenge our young players when they are performing at a level where it's not certain that they're being challenged, it's up to us to make sure that they're being challenged," Boston general manager Ben Cherington said.

Betts continued to play well in Pawtucket. He played a majority of his games in center field for the team, as the Red Sox continued to figure out where his eventual spot on the major league roster might be.

Remarkably, after only a month in Triple-A baseball, the Red Sox decided it was time to see how well he could do in the major leagues. In late June 2014, manager Kevin Boles of Pawtucket called Betts after a game and told him to return to the team's home park. That puzzled the young outfielder until he met Boles in his office.

Although he didn't know it, Betts's time in the minor leagues was almost over. Mookie Betts had been called up to the major leagues. "I kinda [*sic*] just looked at him," Betts told MassLive.com. "I thought I was going to be a lot more excited than I was but I was like, 'All right,' and started packing my stuff. It seemed like everyone else was a lot more excited than I was. I don't know if it was because I was nervous or something." Mookie Betts was on his way to a record-breaking career.

The High School Coach

Minor league baseball players know what to do when they are told they are going to the major leagues: reach for the telephone. Playing at their sport's highest level is the fulfillment of a lifelong dream for most, and athletes can't wait to share it with those who helped make it possible. It's a wonderful moment.

One night in June 2014, the phone of Overton High School baseball coach Mike Morrison rang at 11:35 p.m., waking him up. He noticed that the call was from Mookie Betts.

"When I answered it those were his first words— 'Coach, I'm going to the big leagues,'" Morrison said. "That's pretty special."

Mookie Betts is the best player ever to call Bill Tucker Field home. He was a standout there as a high school player in Nashville.

Most athletes in that situation have one thing in common. They don't sleep. Morrison discovered Betts was no exception when they exchanged text messages the next morning.

"I asked him if he got any sleep and he just kind of said, 'No, not a whole lot,'" Morrison said. "So I know he was excited. Heck, I was excited for him. After I talked to him I had a hard time settling down myself."

The veteran coach doesn't take any credit for Betts's success in baseball.

"The best thing I ever did was get out of his way," Morrison said to MassLive.com. "He is the best we've had. We have had some talented players but never with the skill sets Mookie brought. We've had bits and pieces of skill sets like that but not the whole packages."

Chapter 3

The Big Stage

Mookie Betts was headed to the major leagues, but he wasn't going to the big city of Boston, Massachusetts, quite yet. Betts's path to the big leagues first led south, to a bigger city. He was going to New York City—to be more specific, Yankee Stadium—to join the Red Sox.

Game One

As the song "New York, New York" goes, if you can make it there, you can make it anywhere. The Yankees have the greatest record of success in baseball history, which makes their playing field the most storied location for the sport in the world. Walk into Yankee Stadium, even in its new structure (the old one was bulldozed after the 2008 season), and you can almost feel the ghosts of such all-time greats as Babe Ruth, Lou Gehrig, Joe DiMaggio, and Mickey Mantle.

There's always pressure surrounding someone's first major league game. The setting in this case didn't make it any easier for Mookie Betts.

Opposite: It didn't take long for Betts to become a spectacular outfielder once he began to play the position regularly.

Betts has been a base-stealing threat since arriving in the major leagues in 2014.

Mookie Betts: Baseball Record-Breaker

The Big Stage

Betts sat on the bench on his first day with the Red Sox. The next day, he was on the lineup card hitting eighth and playing right field. It would be only the third time in his professional career that he would play in that outfield spot; Betts had been a center fielder in the minors. Meanwhile, the attendance for that game in Yankee Stadium was 48,124—with a few million more watching ESPN's *Sunday Night Baseball*.

Betts wasn't just another ex-minor leaguer on that night. He represented the hope of a better future for the Red Sox and their fans.

Boston had won the World Series in 2013, a memorable ride in which everything seemed to go right. However, the team's luck flipped at the start of 2014. A ten-game losing streak in mid-May had pushed Boston out of contention. They were seven games out of first place when Betts made his debut. It was necessary to reduce the buildup surrounding Betts's arrival.

"He isn't looked on as the savior for the Red Sox," manager John Farrell said. "It's a quick ascent, no doubt about it. The time has come, as has Mookie."

Every major league player remembers every detail of his first game, and Betts would be no exception. "It was great," the twenty-one-year-old Betts said after the contest. "My first at-bat I had a little jitters. But once I saw the first pitch, it was the same game. For the first game, it was a real incredible atmosphere."

The outfielder grounded into a double play in his first at-bat but singled up the middle in the fourth inning for his first major league hit. His stay on the bases was a short one, as he was caught stealing. "They told me, don't change anything, so I'll take that here and try to be aggressive and steal bases," Betts told the *Boston Globe*. Betts finished the game 1 for 3 with a walk, and he just missed a sinking liner that Ichiro Suzuki turned into a triple. The Red Sox beat the Yankees 8–5 and moved six games out of first in the division. Boston would never again be that close to first place for the rest of the season.

Some Early Struggles

Betts hit his first home run in the major leagues on July 2, 2014. It came off Carlos Villanueva of the Cubs, but it couldn't prevent a 16–9 loss in Fenway Park. Betts provided a peak of his potential on July 9 against the Chicago White Sox. His ground ball between shortstop and third base was fielded by Alexei Ramirez, whose throw to first was too late to catch the speedy Betts. The Red Sox rookie then noticed that Chicago second baseman Gordon Beckham had moved to back up a throw at first, and he saw second base open. Betts ran for second and made it successfully. It was an electric moment.

"At the time, I was screaming, 'What the heck are you doing?'" Farrell said. "But he read the play accurately, and the aggressiveness is combined with some overall awareness, and that's the thing you see for a young guy that's really exciting."

Even Betts wasn't able to conquer the major leagues immediately, though. At the All-Star break in July, he was hitting .235 and was sent back to Pawtucket. Betts came back up on August 1, and he returned to the minors again on August 7. To his credit, he kept hitting while in the minors.

Finally, it was back to the Red Sox on August 18. Betts played that night in Fenway Park against the Los Angeles Angels. If you don't count injury rehabilitation assignments to the minors, Betts was ready to say goodbye to his days in Pawtucket. He left Triple-A

Betts's speed, judgment, and throwing ability have made him one of the best outfielders in the American League.

Mookie Betts: Baseball Record-Breaker

ball with a .346 batting average for the season with 11 home runs and 33 stolen bases.

Betts more or less played out the rest of the season quietly. The Red Sox were hopelessly out of the playoff race by then and eventually fell into last place. Still, Betts showed that he was starting to figure out major league pitching in the final weeks of the season, lifting his batting average for the season to .291 in 52 games and showing power and speed in the process. That included a .310 batting average in the leadoff spot in the batting order.

The Red Sox had been paying attention to that last statistic. Boston had lost Jacoby Ellsbury, its leadoff hitter in the order, to free agency after the 2013 championship season. The Red Sox tried several people in that spot in 2014, but Betts looked like the best choice to take it in 2015. "He's clearly a candidate for us," Farrell said. "Jacoby did such a great job for us for a number of years, and when he signed elsewhere, we went through a little bit of a search to get those skills and that on-base/speed combination to be a little bit of a base-stealing threat. They are rare. Some strength and speed combination doesn't come along with a lot of guys in the big leagues."

Hitting First

The Red Sox opened the 2015 season in Philadelphia, Pennsylvania. The first batter of their season was, sure enough, Betts. Boston couldn't have asked for a better start to a new season. Betts went 2 for 4 with a home run off Philadelphia Phillies ace Cole Hamels. Those two were linked in the off-season; there had been talk that the Red Sox might want to trade Betts for Hamels in an attempt to add a top pitcher to their staff.

It didn't take long for Betts to feel comfortable in the field. The outfielder had three great plays in the month of April alone, showing that he had a chance to become one of the game's elite outfielders.

In New York on April 12, Betts came racing in from center field to rob a batter of what looked like a sure run-scoring single. Then, the Red Sox player got up and lobbed the ball to second base to complete an inning-ending double play. A day later, in Boston's home opener, Betts timed his leap perfectly to rob Bryce Harper of Washington of a homer over the right-center field fence.

Finally, on April 29 against Toronto, Devon Travis hit a screaming line drive into deep center field. Betts raced back, raised his glove, jumped in the air, made the catch, landed on the dirt, and bumped his head against the wall. Then, he held up the ball in his glove to make sure everyone knew the batter was out. "I'm out there doing drill work every day," Betts said to MLB.com. "Credit to [first-base coach Arnie Beyeler] coming out there to work with me. The whole coaching staff, and even in the minors, those guys are working with me a lot. Just happy to be here."

Betts's bat also came through in that win against the Blue Jays. His single in the bottom of the ninth gave Boston a 6–5 win and was his first career walk-off hit. The young player had another special day on May 5. His sixth-inning home run broke up a no-hitter by Tampa Bay's Drew Smyly. Then, in the eighth inning, Betts added another home run in Boston's 2–0 victory. Betts, at 22 years (and 210 days) old, became the youngest player in Red Sox history ever to hit two home runs in one game.

The season wasn't all positive for Betts. He had a couple of minor injuries, one of which came in a game on June 12. He crashed into an outfield wall at Fenway Park and had to leave the game. Betts missed a couple of other contests, and he used the time to think about what his season had been like to that point. He was hitting only .237, not

Mookie Betts takes another trip around the bases as part of a three-homer game against Arizona in 2016.

The Big Stage

up to his standards. Betts talked with some of the team's veterans, like David Ortiz, Dustin Pedroia, and Shane Victorino. They told him to keep working hard because they could see his potential to do better.

"I compared him to 'Cutch' early in his career from what I remember watching Andrew McCutchen," Victorino said of Betts. "And yeah, that is a big guy to put you up against, but I feel Mookie can become that guy, can become that catalyst, become a team leader, by being an electrifying player."

Betts's bat warmed up in the next month, as his average jumped to .277. The path to success is never a straight line and usually includes some wrong turns. Still, Betts finished strongly to have a successful first full season.

The outfielder finished with a .291 batting average; he had the exact same average in 2014. It came with 42 doubles, 8 triples, 18 home runs, and 77 runs batted in. As one analyst put it, if someone threw the ball over the plate to Betts, he hit it very hard. In the field, the biggest complaint about his game was that he kept running into walls. That aggressive approach to fielding needed to be quieted a bit. Still, his speed and arm were assets. Add it up, and the twenty-two-year-old looked like one of the game's best young players.

By the end of the 2015 season, Red Sox fans were thinking back forty years to 1975 when another great young outfielder joined the team. Fred Lynn was the American League's Rookie of the Year and MVP that season. Lynn had more power and more experience in the outfield, but just for Betts to be linked with Lynn showed how well his first full season went.

Betts's arrival as a major league regular was one of the few high points of a mediocre season for the Red Sox. They finished 78–84, fifth and last in the American League East. The signings of free agents Hanley Ramirez and Pablo Sandoval didn't work well, and they didn't have a pitcher win more than eleven games. The losing record wasn't good enough for a franchise that had been a frequent playoff contender for the past few decades, including championships in 2004, 2007, and 2013.

Turning the Page

The Red Sox still had some reason for optimism as the calendar flipped to the 2016 season. Dave Dombrowski had been named the team's president of baseball operations the previous August, and he was ready to put his imprint on the roster. Boston spent $217 million to sign pitcher David Price to a seven-year contract. The Red Sox also had some of the best young players in baseball who were about ready to make an impact. Xander Bogaerts and Jackie Bradley looked ready to join Betts in the lineup.

Betts's 2015 season also had an unexpected benefit. The Red Sox had a good young outfielder in the minor leagues named Manuel Margot. However, his eventual path to the majors looked blocked by Betts and Bradley. Therefore, Boston felt comfortable in trading Margot to the Padres in a deal that brought the Red Sox Craig Kimbrel, one of the best relief pitchers in baseball. The team also convinced slugger David Ortiz to play one more season before retiring.

There was plenty of optimism in Boston, then, as the season opened. Adding to the good feelings was the belief that Betts could be an even better, more consistent player in 2016 than he was the year before. If Betts needed proof that his other athletic skills were in good form, he proved it on the bowling lanes shortly before the start of spring training. He rolled a pair of perfect games.

Betts got the MLB season off to a great start. On opening day,

Betts showed signs in the first game of 2016 that he was about to become one of baseball's best players.

he hit a home run for the second straight year—the youngest player to do that for the Red Sox in one hundred years. Betts also made a leaping catch to rob Rajah Davis of an extra-base hit to right field. It added up to a 6–2 win over the Cleveland Indians. After the game, Ortiz was asked what his reaction was to Betts's play in the opener. He replied simply, "Superstar."

The Red Sox and Betts started the season relatively slowly but heated up a bit in May. The schedule called for a visit to Baltimore, Maryland, at the end of the month, and all of a sudden, Betts found his home-run swing. He hit home runs in the first, second, and seventh innings—three in all—to run his total to 12 for the season at that point. On June 1, Betts hit two more home runs, becoming the first player ever to hit home runs in the first two innings in consecutive games. The outfielder also tied a major league record with the five home runs in two games. "They're just going over the fence right now," Betts said of the power outburst. "I see myself as a gap-to-gap doubles hitter."

Betts's batting average moved up throughout the first half of the season. It went past .300 for the first time in 2016 on July 10. That must have put Betts in a good mood when he went to the All-Star Game for the first time a few days later—and as a starter, no less. "Just shows how much work I've put in," Betts said at the time. "I go out, I do a bunch of work in the outfield, and try to be the best I can be in right field. And I think it shows it's starting to pay off."

The outfielder went 1 for 2 in a game with the sport's best players. His All-Star Game performance didn't help win him the Player of the Month Award for the American League, but some other numbers did—a .368 batting average with 5 home runs. Then on August 14, Betts had yet another three-homer game—this time against Arizona. He was the first Red Sox player since Ted Williams (in 1957) to have a pair of such games in one season. Once again, the first two homers came in the first two innings.

"It's pretty spectacular when you see the first couple of innings—this is the third time this year that he's had home runs in the first couple innings of a ballgame," Red Sox manager John Farrell said about his right fielder. "Second time that he's hit three home runs in a game. Just electric bat speed—against a very good pitcher in [Zack] Greinke."

His Place in the Record Book

Betts still had another big day left in his season. He recorded his 200th hit in a game on September 20 against Baltimore—the second Boston player in history (the first was Johnny Pesky in 1942) to reach that number before the age of 24. Also, Betts became the first player since 2012 (with Miguel Cabrera of Detroit) to have 200 hits, 100 runs scored, and 100 runs batted in for a season.

"I'm proud of him," Pedroia said. "He's been great, obviously, ever since he's come up. He's continued to get better in every aspect of his game. He can help us in a ton of ways. He's pretty special."

Betts and the rest of the Red Sox saved their best month for last, going 19–8 in September to turn a tight pennant race in the American League East into a division championship by a comfortable margin. Boston finished with 93 wins, 15 more than the previous season. Betts finished with a .318 batting average, 31 home runs, 113 runs batted in, and 26 stolen bases. Almost all of his numbers ranked with the league's best.

Unfortunately, Betts and Boston couldn't continue that level of play in the postseason. The Cleveland Indians swept the Red Sox in three straight games, and Betts hit only .200. Once the World Series had ended, it was time for Major League Baseball to announce its individual honors for the 2016 season. Certainly Betts belonged

Mookie Betts: Baseball Record-Breaker

Betts has looked comfortable in the All-Star Game for multiple years in a row.

in the conversation as one of the best players in the American League. "Just having my name buzzed around with David Ortiz and Mike Trout, and some of those names—that's a blessing," Betts said. "Those guys are the best in the game. And no matter whether I win it or I lose it, just the fact I was in the MVP conversation, it's definitely something I'm happy with."

Trout beat out Betts for the MVP honor that time, the second such award for the Los Angeles Angel in his career. Trout was very gracious in describing the player just behind him in the voting. "What an unbelievable player and person," Trout said. "I got to know him a little bit. He's special. He's great for the game. A lot of people ask me about the young guys coming up, and for him to have a year like that, it was just unbelievable. I talked to a bunch of guys on the Red Sox that play with him and they say he's one of the best they've been around. He's a special talent, and it's going to be a fun battle hopefully the next 10 to 15 years."

It didn't take long to wonder how good Betts could become in the 2017 season. After all, he would only be twenty-four years old—younger than the age when many players reach their prime. That season, though, saw a small step backward instead of another step forward. The outfielder was still good in a number of ways but not as good as the season before. For example, Betts was hitting .356 on April 18. That was the day that he hit his first home run of the season and drove in his fourth and fifth runs of 2017. Betts's batting average started a slow decline the next day. He fell below .300 for good on May 14, and he didn't hit his 10th home run until June 14.

Not Quite as Good

The news wasn't all bad. On July 2, Betts went 4 for 6 as he hit

2 home runs and drove in 8 runs. That was the day he was named to play in the All-Star Game for the second time, and he was named to replace Trout in the starting lineup when Trout was injured. Meanwhile, the Red Sox were back in the middle of the pennant race. Still, the season felt a little different without Betts providing a constant offensive spark like he had done in 2016.

"Last year could be arguably the best year I have in my career," Betts told WEEI Radio. "I'm a realist and I know it ain't getting much better than that. When am I going to hit 30 home runs again? I don't know if I ever will. When am I ever going to hit .320 again? I don't know if I ever will."

Betts's batting average dropped into the .260s in mid-August and stayed there for virtually all of the rest of the season. He finished with 24 home runs and 102 runs batted in, and he was 6th in the voting for Most Valuable Player. Still, most analysts thought Betts had been unlucky in 2017. His batting average for balls put in play dropped 54 points from 2016, a sign that he was hitting the ball right at opposing fielders throughout the season.

The Red Sox won 93 games and the American League East title for the second straight season. However, they fell short in the first round of the playoffs once again, losing to the Houston Astros. That wasn't good enough for the Red Sox management, and Farrell—who had won three division titles and a World Series title in five seasons as manager—was fired. "As the season wore on and we got down to the final weeks, maybe there was a little bit of a gut feeling, that you know what, this might be taking place, and it did," Farrell said after his dismissal.

The Red Sox promised to be different under a new manager in 2018. No one could have guessed just how different the season turned out to be.

Mookie's Rival

If Mookie Betts wants to be considered the best baseball player in the world, he'll have to beat out some very tough competition. Mike Trout has had that title for the past few years, and he's not going away. It's fair to say that Trout started to play like a future Hall of Fame star shortly after arriving in the major leagues, and only the best of the best can say that.

Trout had a head start when it came to baseball, as his father, Jeff, was a fifth-round draft choice of the Minnesota Twins. Mike was a star at Millville Senior High School in New Jersey, and he was taken 25th in the first round of the 2009 MLB draft. A little more than a year later, Trout was considered by some the best prospect in baseball. By the summer of 2011, the outfielder was on the Angels' roster.

In 2012, Trout bloomed as an outstanding player at the age of twenty. He won the Rookie of the Year Award, and he finished second in the voting for Most Valuable Player. Since then, Trout has been consistently exceptional. He won MVP trophies in 2014 and 2016, and he was never lower than sixth in the voting in the first seven years of his career.

Trout also earns points for character, adding to his reputation. ESPN's Buster Olney said, "Mike Trout is widely regarded as baseball's best player, and you'd be hard-pressed to find a player who is more universally liked than Trout."

Mike Trout is often said to be the best player in baseball.

That Championship Season

The Boston Red Sox weren't satisfied with only winning their division in 2016 and 2017. They wanted to do better, particularly in October. Therefore, they spared no expense as they prepared for the 2018 season, becoming the biggest spenders in baseball.

The biggest addition was the signing of free agent J. D. Martinez, one of the sport's most feared home-run hitters. With Mookie Betts and Andrew Benintendi—a strong, young left fielder—set for the top of the batting order, Martinez figured to drive in plenty of runs. Power had been a weakness in the Red Sox lineup in 2017.

The team didn't know it during spring training, but the Red Sox were about to begin the best season since the team was born in 1903.

Change at the Top

Boston also had a new manager. Alex Cora was considered one of the smartest players in baseball during a fourteen-year career. After retirement, he became a broadcaster for four years, and then he was

Opposite: Everyone in Boston loves a parade—especially when it features Mookie Betts and the World Series championship trophy!

the bench coach for the Houston Astros in 2017. Cora said when he was hired that he wanted his team to be aggressive at the plate. He commented in a 2017 news conference on his managerial style for the coming season:

> Offensively, everybody loves the homers—we get it. But I think the key of the offense is to have a consistent approach, hunting pitches you can do damage with. First pitch or a 2-0 pitch. Sometimes the first pitch available is the one you can do damage on, so we're going to have guys ready to do damage early in the count, regardless.

Boston's first game came on March 29 and was greeted with great expectations. For a while, it looked as if Boston would get off to a flying start. Pitcher Chris Sale allowed only one hit in six innings of work, and Eduardo Nuñez hit an inside-the-park home run. The Red Sox had a 4–0 lead entering the bottom of the eighth. What could go wrong?

The answer: Plenty could—and did—go wrong. The Tampa Bay Rays scored six runs in the inning and claimed a 6–4 win. It was a discouraging outcome, but Boston bounced back the next day to win, 1–0, behind pitcher David Price. It was an early lesson about what this Red Sox team was like—it did not let adversity linger.

The Red Sox won their next game of the season, and the next one, and the next one. In fact, they won nine in a row. Win number nine came on April 10, a 14–1 thrashing of the New York Yankees. That included one of the biggest days in Betts's career. He went 4 for 4, scored 5 runs, and hit a grand-slam home run. Betts became the second player in history to have four hits, five runs, and four

Alex Cora spent fourteen years in the major leagues as a player before moving on to a second career in coaching and managing.

RBIs in a game against the Yankees; the other was Ken Griffey Jr. of Seattle, in 1996. Apparently, Cora's message had reached Betts. "A slugger leading off, he's going to make contact," Cora said to the Associated Press. "But now he understands that he can do damage in the strike zone."

The winning streak ended a day later, but Boston wasted no time starting a new one. The team was still winning when Betts showed off his home-run power. After missing a few games with a foot injury, the outfielder had three homers in a win over the Los Angeles Angels. That made him the third player in major-league history younger than twenty-six to have three games with three home runs. Ralph Kiner and Boog Powell were the others. "It's pretty fun," Betts said after the game. "Any time you can kind of do something like that, it's huge to help the team. I just ride the wave."

An Amazing Month

The Red Sox won three more games after that to make it eight in a row. They had a 17–2 record after beating Oakland on April 20, with nine of those wins coming by at least four runs. It was the best nineteen-game start in franchise history. "They're doing something special, let's be honest," Cora said to the Associated Press. "There are a lot of people watching the team now, and there are a lot of people talking about the team. You can't help it. You flip the channels and they're talking about what's going on."

The Red Sox finally cooled off a little by the end of April, finishing the month with a 21–7 record. Betts had a .344 batting average at that point, and he would stay around that level for the rest of the season. However, he wasn't done displaying his home-run swing.

On May 2, Betts hit three home runs in a win over Kansas City.

Betts's home runs provided some of the most exciting moments of Boston's 2018 season.

That gave him the league lead in home runs with eleven. Maybe more importantly, Betts took the franchise record for three-homer games from Hall of Famer Ted Williams. Anytime you erase something in the record book by Williams, you've done something special. "It's pretty cool," Betts said to the Associated Press. "He hit .400 in a year and did a whole bunch of things I haven't done. Just to know my name is amongst his is pretty cool."

On May 21, Betts led all major league players in batting average, slugging percentage, home runs, total bases, extra-base hits, doubles, and runs scored. Talk immediately started that he could win the MVP Award.

By June, Betts and the rest of the Red Sox realized that the New York Yankees were going to be good in 2018 as well. On July 1, the teams were tied in the standings, and both had won about two out of every three games they had played. Then, the Red Sox piled up 10 wins in a row, and the Yankees trailed them for the rest of the season.

In that stretch, Betts hit his 22 home run of the season—and the 100th of his career—on July 6 against Kansas City. He was only the fourth Boston player to reach that number before the age of twenty-six. The others were Tony Conigliaro, Ted Williams, and Jim Rice. A few days later, Betts was back in the starting lineup for the All-Star Game.

Later that month, one particular at-bat on July 12 caught the imagination of Boston's baseball fans. Betts was hitting with the bases loaded against Toronto's J. A. Happ. He fouled off seven straight pitches to keep his at-bat alive, and then he homered for a grand slam. Betts was so happy that he tripped slightly rounding first base. "Since I've been in the big leagues, that's probably the most excited that I've been," Betts said.

Burying Yankee Hopes

The Red Sox welcomed the Yankees back to Fenway Park at the start of August for a four-game series. It was a chance for New York to get back in the division race, since the Yankees trailed Boston by 5.5 games at the start of the matchup. The Red Sox set the tone in the first game, as Steve Pearce hit three home runs in a 15–7 romp. Boston also won the next three games to take a 9.5-game lead, essentially wrapping up the division title. Betts went 7 for 16 (.438) at the plate in those four games.

Even when the Red Sox lost in 2018, Betts sometimes had remarkable moments. It could be in the form of a great catch, as he seemed to grab everything in sight while roaming spacious right field in Fenway Park. Sometimes it would be while hitting, like the game on August 9 in Toronto. The Blue Jays won that contest, but Betts hit for the "cycle"—a single, double, triple, and home run in the same game, which only happens in all of baseball a few times each year.

"You expect greatness with him every night," Cora said after the game. "That was cool to see."

The Red Sox kept winning for the rest of the season, going 18–9 in August and 15–11 in September when they could afford to rest some of their regulars for the postseason to come. Even so, they finished with a franchise-record 108 victories against only 54 losses. Betts won the batting title in the American League with a .346 average. Betts also led all players in runs scored (129) and topped right fielders in fielding percentage (.996).

The talk about Betts as the American League's MVP had never stopped through the end of September. "Unbelievable. An MVP-type season," Martinez said about Betts to MLB.com. "I don't know how to say it, but he's been that player that's really stepped up for us, all the way around, and he's consistent, he grinds, he sets a really good example, on the field and in the clubhouse." Meanwhile, Cora made his opinion known to his outfielder. "He repeatedly tells me, there is no doubt you're the best player in the league," Betts said.

Rivalry Renewed

The Red Sox's opponent in the first round of the playoffs was the Yankees. The teams hadn't met in the postseason since 2004, when Boston rallied from a deficit of three games to none to eliminate the Yankees in historic fashion. In 2018, the Yankees had won 100 games, an impressive number, and figured to be a very difficult test for Boston.

Almost anything can happen in such a small number of games during the playoffs. That was the case in 2018, as Betts struggled with his bat. However, other strong players emerged for the Red Sox on an almost nightly basis.

Betts had a double and a run scored in the opener of the best-of-five series at Fenway Park. The Red Sox jumped out to a 5–0 lead and hung on for a 5–4 victory. Then, the Yankees cruised to a 6–2 win in Game Two to even the series and had the next two games on their home field of Yankee Stadium.

Again, Boston showed its resilience. The Red Sox had a 10–0 lead in the fourth inning and went on to win 16–1. Brock Holt hit for the cycle in piling up five hits, while Betts had two hits and two runs scored. That set up a must-win game for the Yankees. The Red Sox took a 4–0 lead and still were ahead by 4–1 entering the bottom of the ninth. New York scored two runs, but Eduardo Nuñez turned a slow ground ball to third into the final out of the game—ending the series.

The Houston Astros were waiting in the next round, and they figured to be a difficult opponent as well. The Astros were the defending World Series champion, and they won 103 games in the regular season. Houston started well in Fenway Park with a 7–2 victory behind ace pitcher Justin Verlander. However, Boston rebounded the next night with a 5–4 win, as Bradley drove in 3 runs and Betts added 2 doubles.

The series shifted to Houston, and Bradley's swing was still working. His grand slam in the eighth inning broke the game open as Boston earned an 8–2 win. Next was Game Four, a memorable contest that took four hours and thirty-three minutes to play nine innings. This was a game in which runners were constantly on base for both teams. A key play in the game was a throw from the outfield.

In the bottom of the eighth, the speedy Tony Kemp hit a line drive down the right-field line. He made the decision to try for a double, but Betts made a perfect throw to catch him in the act. Coincidentally, Kemp and Betts played on the same team when they were teenagers. The Red Sox had some nervous moments from there but still won, 8–6. The victory set the stage for Boston's series-clinching victory, a 4–1 decision. "We got four more wins," David Price said after the game. "That was very, very special, absolutely. But we want more."

Los Angeles vs. Boston

The Red Sox were back in the World Series, a relatively common occurrence in this century. They had participated in the Fall Classic three other times since 2004 and won each of them in fewer than seven games. This time, their opponent was the Los Angeles

Mookie Betts: Baseball Record-Breaker

Mookie's home run in Game Five of the World Series helped the Red Sox finish off the Dodgers.

Dodgers; it was the first Dodgers–Red Sox series since 1916 (although the Dodgers played in Brooklyn then and were known as the Robins).

Betts set the tone for the series in his first at-bat in the bottom of the first in Game One. He singled to center field off star pitcher Clayton Kershaw, and then he immediately stole second. It led to a 2–0 Boston lead. "It was important for us to score first and kind of put some pressure on them," Betts said.

The Dodgers tied the game, 3–3, by the fifth inning, but the Red Sox rebounded with two in the fifth and scored three more in the seventh on a pinch-hit homer by Nuñez. Boston had an 8–5 win. A day later, Martinez's two-run single in the fifth snapped a tie game and the Red Sox had a 4–2 win.

The series had not featured much drama to that point, but Game Three saw more than enough thrills. The game lasted seven hours and twenty minutes and went eighteen innings, both World Series records. Dodgers first baseman David Freese points out that he had never seen a game like that because no one had ever seen a game like that.

The contest finally ended when Max Muncy homered to give the Dodgers their first win. The home run came off Nathan Eovaldi, who threw ninety-seven pitches in his third relief performance in four days. Eovaldi's effort brought teammate Rick Porcello to tears. Betts was hitless in seven at-bats.

Cora called a team meeting to remind his players not to hang their heads after a loss. "We just played one of the greatest games in World Series history. Red Sox ... Dodgers ... Dodger Stadium ... World Series ... And the way you competed is something all of us should be very proud of," he said, according to *Sports Illustrated*.

"This is a great team. This was a great game. And you guys proved it tonight." Then, everyone in the room gave Eovaldi a long hug to show appreciation for his effort.

Porcello later said that the team was in low spirits after losing an eighteen-inning game, but after the meeting, the players had changed their attitude completely.

Suitably motivated, the Red Sox again bounced back from adversity the next day. Boston rallied to take Game Four by a score of 9–6. A day later, Pearce hit a home run in the top of the first to give Boston a 2–0 lead, and that's all the offense the team needed. Price pitched superbly. Betts, who had been taking extra batting practice to sharpen his swing, contributed with a solo home run in the sixth.

When Chris Sale finished striking out the last batter in the bottom of the ninth, the Red Sox were 5–1 winners—and champions of the baseball world.

The Red Sox finished 2018 with 119 victories in all—108 in the regular season and 11 more in the postseason as part of an 11–3 performance. Only two teams had won more games in a calendar year—the 1998 Yankees (125 wins) and the 2001 Mariners (120 wins). They never faced an elimination game in the postseason. It was quite clear at season's end that the best team in baseball—and one of the best ever—won the World Series.

"It's amazing. It's a dream come true," Betts told Fox Sports. "A. C. [Alex Cora] told us from the first day of spring training that we could do it. We believed in him and he believed in us."

Betts was happy to show off baseball's most important trophy right after the end of the 2018 World Series.

Mookie Betts: Baseball Record-Breaker

Quotes About Mookie

"He's probably one of the few guys, every time I see him hit, I think he's going to hit a homer. It's just that presence that he has in the batter's box."
— Xander Bogaerts, teammate

"He gives you a threat even as the game begins. He's an exciting player."
— John Farrell, former MLB pitcher, coach, and manager

"Special player, special player … He's definitely up there with the upper-echelon players in this league. He's just fantastic—talented, athletic, quick hands, great power, good swing."
— Kansas City Royals manager Ned Yost

"Mookie goes two days without getting things done the way he likes it and he starts going crazy. Sometimes, people believe that you only learn from the veterans. No. You learn from guys like him. Me watching him acting like that, me being the veteran, I was like, 'Man, I like that.'"

—David Ortiz, former teammate

"I'm ecstatic about it. Who would have thought, at 26 years old, this boy would be in the World Series?"

—Betts's mother, Diana Collins

"It's how he is in the clubhouse, how people respect him, how he provides leadership. He plays the game hard. He represents the organization in the right way, and that's the type of guy you want. He was tremendous."

—Dave Dombrowski, Red Sox president of baseball operations

Going Forward

ookie Betts played baseball for the longest period possible in 2018—through the last game of the World Series—and finished on October 28 with a championship ring. If he thought at some point he'd have the chance to exhale a little bit once the off-season arrived, he was mistaken.

The peace and quiet lasted a little more than a week. The Red Sox wrapped up the championship on October 28, and on November 6, he and partner Brianna Hammonds became the parents of a baby girl named Kynlee. Betts announced the birth on Instagram with this caption: "Never knew what unconditional love meant or how it felt until I met this little princess. Nov 6th 2018 is a day I'll never forget." Mookie and Brianna had a winter of late-night feedings and diaper changing ahead of them. Betts later said, "Kynlee, I do want to thank you for the two hours of sleep I get every night."

No one is completely ready for the arrival of a first child. Betts had to balance those duties with an off-season full of honors.

Opposite: No one can say Mookie didn't show up in style when he came to a banquet to accept the American League's Most Valuable Player Award.

Tributes and Awards

The day before Kynlee's arrival, Betts won a Gold Glove as one of the best fielders in the American League for the third straight season. On the same day, Betts was picked as one of the three finalists for the American League's Most Valuable Player Award.

A little more than a week later, Betts won the MVP trophy. Betts received twenty-eight of thirty first-place votes, turning the election into a runaway. The hardware went on his shelf right next to the Heart and Hustle Award from the Major League Baseball Players Alumni Association, which goes to the player who "best embodies the values, spirits and traditions of baseball."

It's not easy to win a league MVP Award. Some of the game's all-time greats who never did were Mariano Rivera, Derek Jeter, Tony Gwynn, Randy Johnson, and Rod Carew. However, Betts might have had the best season by a Red Sox player since Carl Yastrzemski's magical 1967 season. Betts became the only American League player to ever win the MVP Award, Gold Glove, and Silver Slugger (best hitter at his position) while playing for a world champion; Mike Schmidt of the 1980 Phillies did this while playing for the National League. Betts came close to capturing the MVP trophy in 2016, so winning it in 2018 was a sweet feeling. "Obviously, I really wanted to win then. Just being in that spot, you don't ever know if you're going to make it back," Betts said to MLB .com. "It's been everything I imagined and more. I think the most important thing is that World Series. That's what kind of sticks in my head first and foremost about the season."

Later in the off-season, Betts finished second in the voting for Male Athlete of the Year from the Associated Press. Basketball's LeBron James was the winner.

It's not easy to win the American League MVP trophy. Ask Mariano Rivera—the great Yankees reliever and Hall of Famer never received that honor.

Financial Reward

Betts's financial reward for his tremendous season came later in the winter. On January 11, 2019, he and the Red Sox avoided salary arbitration by agreeing to a $20 million contract for the upcoming season. That almost doubled his 2018 salary of $10.5 million. Betts was clearly on his way to megastardom, with the riches and attention that come with it. David Howard, a field coordinator for the Red Sox who had been working with Betts since the day he signed, even admitted he underestimated the young player when he first saw him.

Howard said at the time Betts started playing professionally that he would be a player who could hit close to .300 with power, had excellent speed, and could field with anyone—and go on to earn $100 million in his career. Four years later, in 2016, Howard told *USA Today* that he was willing to admit his mistake. "I was wrong, totally wrong," said Howard, who left the Red Sox organization in 2018. "He's going to make $300 million. At least."

No matter how much Betts earns, there's little doubt that he'll be putting it to good use. He's participated in several events to raise money for a variety of good causes. One such gesture resulted in a great deal of publicity, and it came right in the middle of the World Series.

Betts had put ex-teammate David Ortiz in charge of ordering food for a postgame party for Betts's family and friends after Game Two of the World Series. Ortiz called a Dominican restaurant and ordered enough food to fill the kitchen in Betts's apartment. Since the group was headed to Los Angeles the next day, disposing of the leftovers became a problem.

Betts led part of the group on that very cold evening to the Boston Public Library, where the city's homeless often gather at night. There, they served the food to those who couldn't afford to buy it for themselves. "They were really kind of surprised," said Betts's mother, Diana. "You have all these people coming toward me—[they wondered] is this a joke? I could see how some of the people weren't really sure if it was real. But I think they felt the genuine kindness from our hearts." Betts declined to comment about the gesture, but best friend Cam Lewis told *Sports Illustrated*, "We didn't think it would be such a big thing. It was just the right thing to do."

Manager Alex Cora found out about the goodwill action through social media. He wasn't surprised. "Awesome," Cora said. "He's a great kid. And not because he plays for me and we've grown together. Since day one when we met, it was January 4. We sat there at the Commonwealth and we talked for like two hours, three hours, and you could see he was a great guy."

Still on a Roll

You'd expect Betts to continue his association with bowling, considering his skill level at the game, and a tie-in with that sport for charity is a natural fit. Betts hosted "Mookie's Big League Bowl" in Boston in 2017. The event included some of Betts's teammates, and it raised more than $150,000 for two New England charities for children—Pitching in for Kids and One Mission. Betts brought in a few professional bowlers for the event—Tommy Jones, Bill O'Neill, Dom Barrett, Tom Daugherty, Chris Via, and Zulmazran Zulkifli—who put on baseball jerseys for the fund raiser.

Speaking of bowling, Betts and his teammate, Tommy Jones, won the CP3 PBA Celebrity Invitational near Houston in February 2019. The event raised money for a foundation started by basketball star Chris Paul.

After winning the World Series, Betts spent a little time relaxing on the bowling lanes for a charity benefit.

At other times, his gestures aren't so obvious or public. Betts wears a wristband on his right wrist that reads "Love Ya Man." That's a saying from the Will to Life Foundation, a charity group that was started by former Red Sox pitcher John Trautwein, who lost a son to suicide. Betts heard Trautwein speak about his charity work while playing in Triple-A baseball, and the message hit home. One of Betts's best friends took his own life right after the end of high school. The Betts family also had been touched by suicide. "It's one of those things where you just never know what's going on in people's lives," Betts told WEEI.com. "You don't want anybody to take their own life. You want people to support and love one another. That's why you try and stop the hatred … understanding that we're all part of this thing called life. You just don't want anybody to do such a thing, especially when there's so much promise in life."

Betts obviously has many years left in his career and plenty of chances for more achievements. He also has a chance for an even greater task—to serve as one of the public faces for Major League Baseball. That means he'll attract attention to the sport as it competes with the rest of the entertainment world. Betts has the skill set to do that, if he stays healthy in the years to come. The star also has the personality for that job. It starts with a smile that can light up a room. "When Mookie's smiling, good things are happening," Cora said.

His good nature is often on display around a ballpark. It was shown to a national television audience in spring training in 2018, when Betts brought a microphone and earpiece to right field to do an on-the-field, during-the-game interview. Betts was telling an ESPN crew something about bowling when a line drive was hit down the right field line. Betts took off for the ball, telling the national television audience, "Uh, oh, I ain't getting this one, boys," he said. The announcing team roared with approval.

Still, a role model can't just be a happy face. He needs to show others what sort of dedication is needed to become one of baseball's best. Betts has done that. "I'm constantly working. It's not all just God-given," he said. "Obviously, He did bless me with everything I have, but I also do work really hard, probably more than others to try and sustain what I have. People may not know, but I honestly am, probably, I know it's kind of weird to say, but I'm probably one of the more hard workers I've ever seen or been around."

Leading the Way

If he could do all of that while attracting African Americans to the game of baseball, so much the better. Participation in baseball in the black community has been dropping for the past several years. Tony Clark, the executive director of the Major League Baseball Players Association, hopes Betts is part of the solution. "To be quite honest, he represents a community that isn't very well-represented in our game," Clark said. He went on to explain Betts's influence on the game:

> Our entire game and our industry are better with Mookie being here. Whether that's on the field or that's off the field. Mookie represents all that's good with our game, and he represents what's been great about our history. What Mookie can do on a field, what he brings to the ballclub, even just as a fan from the outside looking in, is something our game desperately needs, has always had and hopefully is going to have more of moving forward.

That leaves us with a difficult question: How good can Mookie Betts be? When he turned twenty-six years old, he was named the Most Valuable Player. Many baseball players peak around the age of twenty-seven, but it was tough to imagine that he could show very much improvement from his performance during the 2018 season. The website baseball-reference.com has a way of comparing players over the ages called "Similarity Scores." It determined that Betts's career statistics had the closest comparison through age twenty-five to Duke Snider, the Hall of Fame center fielder for the Dodgers. Betts's numbers also resembled three great Red Sox outfielders—Manny Ramirez, Carl Yastrzemski, and Jim Rice.

Some are willing to take it a step further. Many have compared outfielder Mike Trout of the Angels to Mickey Mantle, the legendary New York Yankees outfielder. Indeed, baseball-reference.com has Trout and Mantle closely linked through age twenty-six. Betts, however, has been connected to another all-time great by one of baseball's top historians. "I personally think that Mookie Betts is, for all practical purposes, a duplicate of Willie Mays," said Bill James, who was a pioneer in the detailed analysis of baseball statistics. "I don't think there is any meaningful difference between Mookie Betts now and Willie Mays in 1956." James said that in the spring of 2018, before all that happened to Betts in 2018.

Mays is considered one of the greatest players in baseball history—perhaps in the top ten. It would be a tall order for Betts to become another Willie Mays. Even so, he's already shown that, on and off the field, he's one of baseball's best.

Mookie Betts can only smile when he thinks about what might happen in the years to come during his baseball career.

Mookie Betts: Baseball Record-Breaker

Mookie Betts Scorecard

Career Highlights: Chosen for his first professional baseball All-Star Game, representing Greenville of the South Atlantic League (2013); reached base in 71 straight games, including five playoff games in the minor leagues (2013–2014); chosen for the All-Star Futures Game (2014); selected for the Major League Baseball All-Star Game (2016, 2017, and 2018); went 129 straight plate appearances without a strikeout (September 12, 2016, to April 19, 2017); stole 30 bases and hit 30 home runs, becoming the second Red Sox player in history to reach both of those numbers in a season (2018); became the first player ever to win baseball's Most Valuable Player, Silver Slugger (hitting), Gold Glove (fielding), batting title, and World Series title in the same season (2018).

Honors and Achievements: Was an honorable mention selection for the Louisville Slugger High School All-American List for baseball (2011); named Most Valuable Player in his region and Player of the Year in Nashville as a senior in high school basketball (2011); accepted a full baseball scholarship from the University of Tennessee, which he later passed up to play professional baseball; selected as the American League's Player of the Year by the Major League Baseball Players Alumni Association (2018); named Player of the Year by the *Sporting News* (2018); won baseball's Heart and Hustle Award, which is given to players who "demonstrate a passion for the game of baseball and best embody the values, spirit and tradition of the game" (2018).

Timeline

October 7, 1992 Markus "Mookie" Lynn Betts is born in Nashville, Tennessee.

November 2010 Betts signs a letter of commitment to attend the University of Tennessee on a baseball scholarship.

June 6, 2011 Betts is drafted in the fifth round of the Major League Baseball draft by the Boston Red Sox.

August 15, 2011 Betts signs a professional contract with Red Sox for $750,000.

Fall 2013 Betts plays in the Arizona Instructional League.

Spring 2014 Betts is assigned to the Double-A Portland Sea Dogs of the Eastern League.

June 30, 2014 Betts plays his first major league game, starting at center field against the Yankees in New York.

July 3, 2014 Betts hits his first big league home run. The baseball was caught in the stands by Chris Lange, who played against Betts in high school baseball.

July 12, 2016 Betts plays in his first Major League Baseball All-Star Game.

November 13, 2017 Betts rolls a perfect 300 game in the Professional Bowlers Association (PBA) World Series of Bowling.

May 2, 2018 Betts sets a Red Sox record for most three-homer games in a career after connecting three times against Kansas City.

August 9, 2018 Betts hits for the cycle (single, double, triple, and home run) during a loss to the Toronto Blue Jays.

September 30, 2018 Betts claims the American League batting championship with a .346 batting average as the regular season comes to an end.

October 28, 2018 Betts and the Red Sox win the World Series, beating the Los Angeles Dodgers four games to one.

November 6, 2018 Betts's daughter, Kynlee, is born.

November 15, 2018 Betts wins the Most Valuable Player Award in the American League.

January 11, 2019 Betts agrees to a $20 million salary for the 2019 season from the Red Sox. He could become a free agent after the 2020 season.

Glossary

advanced placement (AP) A program that allows high school students to take college-level courses and examinations. Universities may give college credits to students who receive excellent test scores in those examinations.

allotment The amount a baseball team is allowed to spend on draft choices in a given year. The exact number of dollars is determined by a number of factors, such as a team's place in the draft order and its number of selections. A tax is placed on a team if it spends more than its limit.

banner A piece of cloth that is specially made to mark some sort of championship in baseball (World Series, league title, division title). It's been a custom for teams for decades to have banners placed somewhere on their home ballpark's grounds—often on the flag pole—after winning a championship.

barrel A nickname for the thickest part of a baseball bat.

batting average The number of hits divided by the number of official at-bats over a given time period. Someone who has a .300 batting average—with three hits in every ten at-bats—is considered to be a very good batter.

bench coach A person who essentially is the top assistant to a baseball manager.

extra-base hits Hits without including singles—in other words, doubles, triples, and home runs.

extra hitter A player who is added to the batting order, which therefore has ten participants instead of the traditional nine. While most baseball leagues use a designated hitter, in which a team member becomes a permanent substitute for the pitcher in the batting order, the extra hitter is most often used in high school baseball and other youth leagues.

Fall Classic A nickname for the World Series.

free agent A professional player who is free to sign a contract with another team after their old contract expires. In baseball, most free agents have either played at least six years in the major leagues or have been released by their former teams.

gap In baseball, the spaces between the three outfielders, in either left-center field or right-center field.

Gold Glove An award given to the top fielders at each position in both the American League and National League. This tradition started in 1957.

infield The inner part of the field of play in baseball.

injury rehabilitation assignment A period of time when a major league player has almost recovered from an injury that has kept him off the playing roster and he needs to play in a few games in the minor leagues to practice his skills before returning to his usual team.

Instructional League A baseball league in Arizona in which professionals play games in September and October in an attempt to improve their skills. Its players are usually just out of high school or college, but sometimes veterans take part in the league when they are recovering from an injury or if they are planning on playing a new position in spring training a few months later.

manager The person who is in charge of the day-to-day operation of a baseball team.

pennant race The ongoing competition during the course of a baseball season to win the division or league championship.

perfect game In bowling, it consists of twelve strikes in a row and results in a score of 300.

professional Someone who earns a living at a particular task. The word is often shortened to "pro" in sports.

rookie A player in their first year. A "rookie league" is filled with first-year players.

Rubik's Cube A puzzle invented by Erno Rubik of Hungary in 1974 that features lines of colored squares that can be moved so each face of the cube is made up of only one color.

salary arbitration A business procedure in baseball in which a player with a certain level of time on a major-league roster and his team both submit a salary offer for the upcoming season to an independent judge. The independent judge then picks one of the offers.

Silver Slugger An award given to the best offensive player at each position for players in both the American League and National League. Mookie Betts won this honor in 2016 and 2018.

Triple-A team The league that is said to be closest to the major leagues in terms of the quality of play. Minor leagues are classified by either Rookie, A, AA, or AAA, depending on the level of play.

walk-off hit A hit in a baseball game that puts the home team ahead in the last inning and therefore ends the game. The losing team must "walk off" the field before it has recorded three outs in the inning.

World Series A group of games between the champions of the American League and National League to determine the best team in baseball. It began in 1903. The first team to win four games out of seven becomes the world champion.

Further Information

Books

Bates, Greg. *Mookie Betts*. Mendota Heights, MN: Focus Readers, 2019.

Drelich, Evan. *The Big 50: Boston Red Sox*. Chicago, IL: Triumph Books, 2018.

Frederick, Jace. *Baseball's New Wave: The Young Superstars Taking Over the Game*. Mendota Heights, MN: Press Box Books, 2019.

Prime, Jim, and Bill Nowlin. *The Boston Red Sox Killer B's: Baseball's Greatest Outfield*. New York, NY: Sports Publishing, 2019.

Sneddon, Rob. *Boston's 100 Greatest Gamers*. Independently published, 2018.

Triumph Books. *The Rest Is History: Boston Red Sox 2018 World Series Champions*. Chicago, IL: Triumph Books, 2018.

Websites

Baseball Reference: Mookie Betts

https://www.baseball-reference.com/players/b/bettsmo01.shtml
This website provides statistics and an overview of Mookie Betts's baseball career.

Boston Red Sox

http://www.redsox.com
The official Boston Red Sox page gives statistics as well as links to articles and videos.

ESPN Biography: Mookie Betts

http://www.espn.com/mlb/player/_/id/33039/mookie-betts
The ESPN website gives an in-depth look at Mookie Betts's background and career highlights.

Major League Baseball

https://www.mlb.com
The official site of Major League Baseball provides news, videos, and statistics on baseball players and teams.

NBC Sports: Boston

https://www.nbcsports.com/boston
The NBC Sports website provides news updates and live streaming on the Red Sox and other teams.

SB Nation: World Series

https://www.sbnation.com/world-series
The SB Nation website provides complete coverage of the World Series.

Videos

2018 Boston Red Sox Postseason Highlights

https://www.youtube.com/watch?v=0jYw91noZK8
The playoffs are condensed into 18 minutes as the Red Sox storm past the Yankees, Astros, and Dodgers to a World Series title.

2018 Champs Stand Out as Greatest Red Sox Team

https://www.mlb.com/redsox/news/2018-world-series-champs-greatest-red-sox-team/c-299908396
This website has a collection of videos made just after Boston defeated the Dodgers to capture the world championship.

2018 MVP Highlights

https://www.youtube.com/watch?v=UOfqr3j-Pzs
This video features a collection of Mookie Betts's career highlights.

2018 World Series Home Run

https://www.youtube.com/watch?v=JatnQxxPjB4
This video shows Mookie Betts hitting a home run in Game Five of the 2018 World Series.

Bibliography

Abraham, Peter. "Mookie Betts Looking Ahead After Receiving
AL MVP Hardware from Baseball Writers." *Boston Globe*,
January 27, 2019. https://www.bostonglobe.com/sports/
redsox/2019/01/27/mookie-betts-receives-mvp-award-from-
baseball-writers-new-york/r2WsoV0Bl0P3brRZwSDpiI/story.
html.

Apstein, Stephanie. "A Quiet Gesture from Mookie Betts During the
2018 World Series Made a Resounding Impact." *Sports Illustrated*,
December 5, 2018. https://www.si.com/mlb/2018/12/05/
mookie-betts-boston-red-sox-feeding-the-homeless-inspirational-
moments.

Baumann, Michael. "The Best Player in Baseball Doesn't Want to Be
a Superstar." The Ringer, March 30, 2017. https://www.theringer.
com/2017/3/30/16045258/mike-trout-doesnt-want-to-be-a-
superstar-los-angeles-angels-mlb-cbb8442702c2.

Bowers, Rachel. "Alex Cora Embraces Opportunity in Baseball-Mad
Boston." Boston.com, November 6, 2017. https://www.boston.
com/sports/boston-red-sox/2017/11/06/alex-cora-formally-
introduced-as-red-sox-manager.

Bradford, Rob. "How Mookie Betts Went from Water Boy to Weight
Lifter." WEEI Radio. Accessed on January 18, 2019. https://weei.
radio.com/articles/column/how-mookie-betts-went-water-boy-
weightlifter.

Bradford, Rob. "Why This Week Means More to Mookie Betts."
WEEI Radio. Accessed on February 1, 2019. https://weei.radio.
com/blogs/rob-bradford/why-week-means-more-mookie-betts.

Browne, Ian. "Betts Claims First AL Batting Title with .346 Average." MLB.com, September 30, 2018. http://wap.mlb.com/bos/news/article/20180930296665228/.

Browne, Ian. "Betts Finishes 2nd to Trout in AL MVP Voting." MLB .com, November 17, 2016. https://www.mlb.com/redsox/news/mookie-betts-in-second-place-for-al-mvp-award/c-209087422.

Browne, Ian. "Betts Wins AL MVP Award." MLB.com, November 15, 2018. https://www.mlb.com/news/mookie-betts-wins-american-league-mvp-award/c-300779614.

Browne, Ian. "Prospect Betts Moves Up to Triple-A." MLB.com, June 3, 2014. https://www.mlb.com/news/red-sox-prospect-mookie-betts-promoted-to-triple-a-pawtucket/c-78042992.

Cafardo, Nick. "Much Excitement as Mookie Betts Makes Debut." *Boston Globe,* June 29, 2014. https://www.bostonglobe.com/sports/2014/06/29/mookie-betts-makes-his-debut-with-red-sox/FWOMtSJIU4MsmCpx4dFU5O/story.html.

Cirillo, Chip. "Mookie Betts Starts Pro Career with Spinners." *Tennessean,* June 27, 2012. https://www.tennessean.com/story/highschoolsports/2012/06/27/mookie-betts-starts-pro-career-with-spinners/5427939.

Cirillo, Chip. "Red Sox Call Up Former Overton Star Mookie Betts." *Tennessean,* June 28, 2014. https://www.tennessean.com/story/sports/preps/2014/06/28/mookie-betts-bostonred-sox-overton/11622817.

DeCosta-Klipa, Nik. "Mookie Betts on His 2016 Season." Boston.com, August 2, 2017. https://www.boston.com/sports/boston-red-sox/2017/08/02/mookie-betts-on-his-2016-season-im-a-realist-it-aint-getting-much-better-than-that.

Doyle, Bill. "Betts Caps Off Special Season." *Providence Journal,* September 30, 2018. https://www.providencejournal.com/sports/20180930/betts-caps-off-special-season.

Dubilo, Ruthi. "Mookie Betts Reflects on How Childhood Car Accident Changed His Life." NESN, September 2014. https://nesn.com/2014/09/mookie-betts-reflects-on-how-childhood-car-accident-changed-his-life.

Golen, Jimmy. "Red Sox Claim More Titles, Beating Yankees 10–2 in Finale." Associated Press, September 30, 2018. https://www.boston.com/sports/boston-red-sox/2018/09/30/red-sox-yankees-records.

Grosnick, Bryan. "Mookie Betts' Breakout Season." Sports on Earth, November 6, 2015. http://www.sportsonearth.com/article/156604172/mookie-betts-bp-boston-roster-recap-red-sox.

Kory, Matthew. "Sudden Superstar." Sports on Earth, May 6, 2014. http://www.sportsonearth.com/article/74403548/boston-red-sox-second-baseman-mookie-betts-minor-league-top-prospect.

Lee, Joon. "Mookie Betts Is Great at Every Sport He's Ever Played." SB Nation, June 30, 2015. https://www.overthemonster.com/2015/6/30/8422417/mookie-betts-dunking-basketballs-and-being-generally-awesome.

Lee, Joon. "The Rise of Mookie Betts." SB Nation, April 24, 2015. https://www.sbnation.com/mlb/2015/4/24/8470493/mookie-betts-red-sox-prospect.

McCaffrey, Jen. "How Did Mookie Betts' High School Coach Handle the Future Red Sox OF?" Mass Live, July 15, 2015. https://www.masslive.com/redsox/index.ssf/2015/07/mookie_betts_high_school_coach.html.

McCaffrey, Jen. "Mookie Betts, also an MVP to Those in Need." The Athletic, October 26, 2018. https://theathletic.com/616496/2018/10/26/mookie-betts-also-an-mvp-to-those-in-need/.

McCaffrey, Jen. "Mookie Betts Sets MLB Record with Five Home Runs in Two Games as Leadoff Hitter." Mass Live. Accessed on June 2, 2016. https://www.masslive.com/redsox/index.ssf/2016/06/mookie_betts_sets_mlb_record_w.html.

McCaffrey, Jen. "The Story of Mookie Betts' Rise from Nashville to Boston Red Sox Franchise Cornerstone." Mass Live, July 15, 2015. https://www.masslive.com/redsox/index.ssf/2015/07/boston_red_sox_mookie_betts.html.

McCaffrey, Jen. "What's Mookie Betts' Real Name?" Mass Live, July 16, 2015. https://www.masslive.com/redsox/index.ssf/2015/07/what_is_mookie_betts_real_name.html.

Mellen, Chris. "2013 Prospect Previews." Sox Prospects, March 6, 2013. http://news.soxprospects.com/2013/03/2013-prospect-previews-watch-list-bats.html.

Nightengale, Bob. "Here's Why the Red Sox's Mookie Betts Deserves to be American League MVP." USA Today, October 5, 2016. https://www.usatoday.com/story/sports/mlb/columnist/bob-nightengale/2016/10/05/mookie-betts-boston-red-sox-playoffs-mvp-boston-david-ortiz/91631630.

Pence, Owen. "'When Mookie's Smiling, Good Things Are Happening.'" Boston Globe, October 14, 2018. https://www.bostonglobe.com/sports/redsox/2018/10/14/mookie-betts-brings-undeniable-energy/adatp3R3UHgf5E4y6z8YYL/story.html.

Phillips, Gary. "From Little League to Boston, Mookie Betts' Mom Has Never Stopped Coaching Him." *Sporting News*, May 13, 2018. http://www.sportingnews.com/us/mlb/news/mookie-betts-mom-red-sox-mothers-day-boston-mom-mvp-stats-diana-benedict-little-league/1o5ntg3jkccx71elsumcw0lx6y.

Reimer, Alex. "Mookie Betts Showed He's Ready to be a Superstar on Opening Day." *Boston Magazine*, April 6, 2016. https://www.bostonmagazine.com/news/2016/04/06/mookie-betts-highlights-red-sox/.

Rexroad, Joe. "The Mookie Betts Story, Starring Nashville and Strong Parents." *Tennessean*, October 12, 2018. https://www.tennessean.com/story/sports/2018/10/12/mookie-betts-red-sox-superstar-nashville-roots-rexrode/1500780002/.

Robinson, Tom. "Overton's Mookie Betts Impressing in Red Sox System." *Tennessean*, May 6, 2014. https://www.tennessean.com/story/sports/2014/05/06/overton-mookie-betts-eastern-league-red-sox/8763523/.

Sanchez, Robert. "Small Ball." ESPN, September 22, 2018. http://www.espn.com/mlb/story/_/id/24741219/mlb-boston-red-sox-slugger-mookie-betts-leading-mlb-little-guy-revolution.

Shirkey, Alec. "Betts Yet? Mookie Makes Another Highlight-Reel Grab." MLB.com, April 29, 2015. https://www.mlb.com/redsox/news/red-sox-center-fielder-mookie-betts-adds-another-highlight-reel-catch-to-resume/c-121283320.

Smith, Christopher. "AL All-Star Starters 2016." Mass Live, July 5, 2016. https://www.masslive.com/redsox/index.ssf/2016/07/al_all-star_starters_mookie_be.html.

Sneddon, Rob. "Boston's 100 Greatest Games." Independently published, 2018.

Triumph Books. *The Rest Is History: Boston Red Sox 2018 World Series Champions*. Chicago, IL: Triumph Books, 2018.

Weitzman, Yaron. "MLB Megastar Mookie Betts Is Rare Master of All Trades." Bleacher Report, November 15, 2016. https://bleacherreport.com/articles/2668544-mlb-megastar-mookie-betts-is-rare-master-of-all-trades.

Weigel, Dan. "The Rise of Mookie Betts." SB Nation, August 1, 2014. https://www.beyondtheboxscore.com/2014/8/1/5960973/the-rise-of-mookie-betts.

Yates, Clinton. "Mookie Betts Is the Superstar Baseball Needs." Undefeated, November 15, 2018. https://theundefeated.com/features/boston-red-sox-mookie-betts-is-the-superstar-baseball-needs.

Index

Page numbers in **boldface** are images.

About the Author

Budd Bailey retired as an editor and reporter in the sports department for the *Buffalo News* in 2017 after working there for more than twenty-three years. Before that, he worked for WEBR Radio in Buffalo, where he was a reporter, talk-show host, and baseball announcer for the broadcasts of the Buffalo Bisons. Bailey currently works as a freelance writer, including a position as a columnist for the website Buffalo Sports Page. The Syracuse University graduate has written nine books for Cavendish Square, including biographies of baseball superstars Jackie Robinson and Ichiro Suzuki, and twelve books in all. Bailey and his wife, Jody, live in Buffalo, New York.